LOVE JOURNAL

by

Cynthia Owen

Love Journal
ISBN: 978-0-9971652-4-1
Copyright © 2018 by Cynthia Owen

All rights reserved. No part of this book may be reproduced in any form without permission in writing from the publisher, except in the case of brief quotations embodied in critical articles or reviews.

All Scripture quotations are from the King James Version of the Bible.

Published by:
JC Owen and Associates, Inc.
3597 E. Monarch Sky Lane, Suite F-240
Meridian, ID 83646

Printed in the United States of America.

Dear Friend,

Love is the most powerful truth on the earth. It is built into each one of us by God.

I'm reminded of the scripture, "There is no fear in love; but perfect love casteth out fear..." (1 John 4:18). When we come to a deeper understanding of the love of God, we gain a different perspective on our lives. We are at peace, and not driven or controlled by fear.

Understanding the love of God means we don't need to worry about being rejected, because we have already been accepted by the Father, who loves us deeply. We understand that we don't need to be perfect, or have to perform in a certain way. We also won't be seeking acceptance by becoming "people pleasers." We know that we have been accepted by God just because he loves us. It's not because of who we are or what we've done, but because of who he is. **God is love.** Coming to know the love of God, and by having this love at the very core of who we are as his children, allows us to live healthy and happy lives.

Love changes everything around us. It will defuse an argument, bring hope to the hopeless, bring peace into difficult circumstances and change the lives of those around us in the most incredible ways. When we create a loving environment to live in every day, we are truly healthier and happier people.

Let the love of God change your thinking and your life. Learn to live a life filled with the love of God. Receive the love that God has for you as you further develop your love for God, for yourself and for those around you. And as you make these changes, you will see and experience the most amazing and powerful force on the earth, which is the love of God.

Many blessings to you,
Cindy

KEYS TO DISCOVERING THE LOVE OF GOD

Discover who your Father in heaven is by reading the Bible. God is love. You can find out about the character of God by reading the word of God.

Learn to take the truths of God's word and live your life according to those truths.

Spend time focusing on the care that God extends toward you in the area of provision. You will see how God loves you and takes care of you every day.

Learn to love yourself for who you are, as God has created you. Take God at his word regarding what he has to say about you, and how you were created in his very image and likeness. Let go of any low self-esteem, or even self-hatred. As you do this, you will begin to feel whole about yourself, and in turn it will become easier to see others for who they are, as God has created them. This will help you to love others.

Become aware of the love of God in others. In doing so, you will see how great the love of God actually is on the earth. As Paul says in Ephesians 3:18-19, "...that you may be able to comprehend with all saints what is the breadth, and length, and depth, and height; and to know the love of Christ, ..."

As you sow seeds of love toward others, it will help to break off any brokenness or resentment that you have experienced as a result of others who did not extend the love of God toward you.

Learn to become a giver. "For God so loved the world that he gave..." (John 3:16); God gave you his most valuable and powerful possession, his only Son, so you could be free. As you give to others, God will reveal to you how his love is at work through your giving.

As you read the Love Journal, my hope is that you will discover a greater sense of the love of God.

LOVE

"I love the Lord, because he hath heard my voice and my supplications."
Psalm 116:1

Insights:
_____
_____
_____
_____
_____
_____
_____
_____
_____
_____
_____
_____
_____
_____
_____
_____
_____
_____
_____

My Declaration: *"Lord, I declare that **I will lift up my voice to you** in a time of need."*

LOVE

"Jesus said unto him, Thou shalt love the Lord thy God with all thy heart, and with all thy soul, and with all thy mind."
Matthew 22:37

Insights:

_____
_____
_____
_____
_____
_____
_____
_____
_____
_____
_____
_____
_____
_____
_____
_____
_____
_____

My Declaration: *"Lord, I declare that I love you, and I will serve you **with my whole heart**."*

LOVE

*"He that covereth a transgression seeketh love;
but he that repeateth a matter separateth very friends."
Proverbs 17:9*

Insights:

My Declaration: *"Lord, I declare that I will not gossip but will **seek love** in all that I do."*

LOVE

*"Consider how I love thy precepts: quicken me,
O Lord, according to thy lovingkindness."
Psalm 119:159*

Insights:

My Declaration: *"Lord, I declare that I love your word, and it keeps me in all my ways."*

LOVE

"Death and life are in the power of the tongue: and they that love it shall eat the fruit thereof."
Proverbs 18:21

Insights:
_____
_____
_____
_____
_____
_____
_____
_____
_____
_____
_____
_____
_____
_____
_____
_____
_____
_____

My Declaration: *"Lord, I declare that I will choose to use my tongue for good and not for evil, and I will enjoy all the benefits that follow."*

LOVE

"But God commendeth his love toward us, in that, while we were yet sinners, Christ died for us."
Romans 5:8

Insights:

My Declaration: *"Lord, I declare that you have **proven your love for me** by sending your Son to die for my sins while I was still a sinner. **I am fully assured** that you are, and always will be, on my side."*

LOVE

*"The Lord preserveth all them that love him:
but all the wicked will he destroy."
Psalm 145:20*

Insights:
_____
_____
_____
_____
_____
_____
_____
_____
_____
_____
_____
_____
_____
_____
_____
_____
_____
_____
_____
_____
_____

My Declaration: *"Lord, I declare that you will preserve me and protect me; you have promised to destroy all of my enemies."*

LOVE

"Herein is love, not that we loved God, but that he loved us, and sent his Son to be the propitiation for our sins."
1 John 4:10

Insights:

My Declaration: *"Lord, I declare that Jesus is my redeemer, and I can trust he is constantly working in my behalf, **helping me to overcome** any weaknesses or fears."*

LOVE

"I love them that love me; and those that seek me early shall find me."
Proverbs 8:17

Insights:
_____
_____
_____
_____
_____
_____
_____
_____
_____
_____
_____
_____
_____
_____
_____
_____
_____
_____
_____
_____
_____

My Declaration: *"Lord, I declare that I will seek you **every day** as I find more and more of your loving kindness."*

LOVE

*"Therefore I love thy commandments above gold;
yea, above fine gold."*
Psalm 119:127

Insights:

My Declaration: *"Lord, I declare that your laws mean more to me than the finest gold;* ***I love your paths of righteousness.****"*

LOVE

"Better is a dinner of herbs where love is, than a stalled ox and hatred therewith."
Proverbs 15:17

Insights:
_____
_____
_____
_____
_____
_____
_____
_____
_____
_____
_____
_____
_____
_____
_____
_____
_____
_____
_____
_____

My Declaration: *"Lord, I declare that I will seek after loving relationships. I will make the choice **to remove myself** from those who are deceitful and unloving."*

LOVE

"O love the Lord, all ye his saints: for the Lord preserveth the faithful, and plentifully rewardeth the proud doer."
Psalm 31:23

Insights:
_____
_____
_____
_____
_____
_____
_____
_____
_____
_____
_____
_____
_____
_____
_____
_____
_____
_____
_____

My Declaration: "Lord, I declare that **I will be found faithful in all of my ways.**"

LOVE

*"But I say unto you which hear, Love your enemies,
do good to them which hate you, bless them that curse you,
and pray for them which despitefully use you."*
Luke 6:27-28

Insights:

_____
_____
_____
_____
_____
_____
_____
_____
_____
_____
_____
_____
_____
_____
_____
_____
_____

My Declaration: *"Lord, I declare that **I will do good** to those who come into my life; I will treat them as you would."*

LOVE

"Ye that love the Lord, hate evil: he preserveth the souls of his saints; he delivereth them out of the hand of the wicked."
Psalm 97:10

Insights:
_____
_____
_____
_____
_____
_____
_____
_____
_____
_____
_____
_____
_____
_____
_____
_____
_____
_____
_____
_____
_____
_____

My Declaration: *"Lord, I declare that I will have nothing to do with evil;* ***I will seek your paths of righteousness,*** *and I will watch your mighty hand deliver me."*

LOVE

"For God hath not given us the spirit of fear; but of power, and of love, and of a sound mind."
2 Timothy 1:7

Insights:
_____
_____
_____
_____
_____
_____
_____
_____
_____
_____
_____
_____
_____
_____
_____
_____
_____
_____
_____

My Declaration: "Lord, I declare that **I will not walk in fear, but I shall remain in faith**. I will be counted among the faithful."

LOVE

*"But let all those that put their trust in thee rejoice:
let them ever shout for joy, because thou defendest them:
let them also that love thy name be joyful in thee."
Psalm 5:11*

Insights:

_____
_____
_____
_____
_____
_____
_____
_____
_____
_____
_____
_____
_____
_____
_____
_____
_____
_____

My Declaration: *"Lord, I declare that I will **put my trust** in you alone. I will praise you with my whole heart."*

LOVE

"A new commandment I give unto you, That ye love one another; as I have loved you, that ye also love one another."
John 13:34

Insights:
_____
_____
_____
_____
_____
_____
_____
_____
_____
_____
_____
_____
_____
_____
_____
_____
_____
_____
_____
_____
_____
_____
_____
_____

My Declaration: *"Lord, I declare that **I will show love** in all that I do. I will extend a hand of blessing to those around me."*

LOVE

"And the Lord direct your hearts into the love of God, and into the patient waiting for Christ."
2 Thessalonians 3:5

Insights:
_____
_____
_____
_____
_____
_____
_____
_____
_____
_____
_____
_____
_____
_____
_____
_____
_____
_____
_____

My Declaration: *"Lord, I declare that you will show me your loving kindness, and give me your patient endurance."*

LOVE

"Love not the world, neither the things that are in the world. If any man love the world, the love of the Father is not in him."
1 John 2:15

Insights:
_____
_____
_____
_____
_____
_____
_____
_____
_____
_____
_____
_____
_____
_____
_____
_____
_____
_____
_____

My Declaration: *"Lord, I declare that I will not love the world, or the things of it, but I will love and seek **you**."*

LOVE

"That Christ may dwell in your hearts by faith; that ye, being rooted and grounded in love, ..."
Ephesians 3:17

Insights:

My Declaration: "*Lord, I declare that I will prayerfully consider your amazing love. **I will be rooted and grounded in you.**"

LOVE

"Hatred stirreth up strifes: but love covereth all sins."
Proverbs 10:12

Insights:

My Declaration: "Lord, I declare that I will **walk in love**, and I will pursue peace."

LOVE

"But let us, who are of the day, be sober, putting on the breastplate of faith and love; and for an helmet, the hope of salvation."
1 Thessalonians 5:8

Insights:
_____
_____
_____
_____
_____
_____
_____
_____
_____
_____
_____
_____
_____
_____
_____
_____
_____

My Declaration: *"Lord, I declare that **I will put on love** and stand strongly as I hope in your salvation."*

LOVE

"I will love thee, O Lord, my strength."
Psalm 18:1

Insights:

My Declaration: *"Lord, I declare that you are my strength and my shield;* ***I put my trust in you.****"*

LOVE

"And this I pray, that your love may abound yet more and more in knowledge and in all judgment;"
Philippians 1:9

Insights:
___
___
___
___
___
___
___
___
___
___
___
___
___
___
___
___
___
___
___
___

My Declaration: *"Lord, I declare that your love will abound more and more in my heart."*

LOVE

"And the grace of our Lord was exceeding abundant with faith and love which is in Christ Jesus."
1 Timothy 1:14

Insights:
_____
_____
_____
_____
_____
_____
_____
_____
_____
_____
_____
_____
_____
_____
_____
_____
_____
_____
_____

My Declaration: *"Lord, I declare that your grace is sufficient **in every way** that I need in my life."*

LOVE

*"Let all those that seek thee rejoice and be glad in thee:
let such as love thy salvation say continually,
The Lord be magnified."*
Psalm 40:16

Insights:
_____
_____
_____
_____
_____
_____
_____
_____
_____
_____
_____
_____
_____
_____
_____
_____
_____

My Declaration: *"Lord, I declare that I will seek you with my whole heart; I will rejoice and be glad in you."*

LOVE

"If ye love me, keep my commandments."
John 14:15

Insights:

My Declaration: *"Lord, I declare that I love you, and I will follow **your paths** and **your ways**."*

LOVE

"For he that will love life, and see good days, let him refrain his tongue from evil, and his lips that they speak no guile:"
1 Peter 3:10

Insights:
_____
_____
_____
_____
_____
_____
_____
_____
_____
_____
_____
_____
_____
_____
_____
_____
_____
_____

My Declaration: *"Lord, I declare that I want to see long life and good days; I choose to keep my tongue from saying evil things, and will always speak true words of life into any situation."*

LOVE

"Let brotherly love continue."
Hebrews 13:1

Insights:

___
___
___
___
___
___
___
___
___
___
___
___
___
___
___
___
___
___
___
___
___
___

My Declaration: *"Lord, I declare that I will continue in brotherly love;* ***I will move away from strife.****"*

LOVE

"For God is not unrighteous to forget your work and labour of love, which ye have shewed toward his name, in that ye have ministered to the saints, and do minister."
Hebrews 6:10

Insights:

My Declaration: *"Lord, I declare that you are the one who rewards me for my work.* **I will look to you** *as my source for all that I need."*

LOVE

"Finally, be ye all of one mind, having compassion one of another, love as brethren, be pitiful, be courteous:"
1 Peter 3:8

Insights:
_____
_____
_____
_____
_____
_____
_____
_____
_____
_____
_____
_____
_____
_____
_____
_____
_____
_____

My Declaration: *"Lord, I declare that I will follow your word by **showing love and compassion** to those around me."*

LOVE

*"And let us consider one another
to provoke unto love and to good works:"
Hebrews 10:24*

Insights:
___

My Declaration: *"Lord, I declare that I will consider those around me; **I will continue doing good** on the earth."*

LOVE

"Let love be without dissimulation. Abhor that which is evil; cleave to that which is good."
Romans 12:9

Insights:

My Declaration: *"Lord, I declare that my love will always be genuine; I will reject evil, and **seek after** that which is good."*

LOVE

"Hold fast the form of sound words, which thou hast heard of me, in faith and love which is in Christ Jesus."
2 Timothy 1:13

Insights:
_____
_____
_____
_____
_____
_____
_____
_____
_____
_____
_____
_____
_____
_____
_____
_____
_____
_____
_____
_____
_____

My Declaration: *"Lord, I declare that my words will be **solid** and **full of faith, love and righteousness**."*

LOVE

"For I am persuaded, that neither death, nor life, nor angels, nor principalities, nor powers, nor things present, nor things to come, nor height, nor depth, nor any other creature, shall be able to separate us from the love of God, which is in Christ Jesus our Lord."
Romans 8:38-39

Insights:

_____
_____
_____
_____
_____
_____
_____
_____
_____
_____
_____
_____
_____
_____
_____
_____
_____

My Declaration: *"Lord, I declare that I am fully convinced:* ***nothing can separate me from you and your love!"***

Other Journals by Cynthia Owen

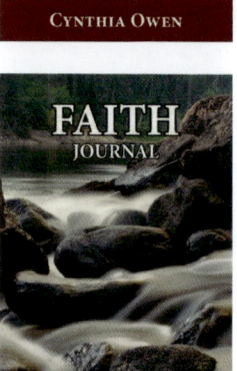

Let's Pray Together

Do you know for certain that when you die, heaven will be your home? If there's any doubt at all, pray this prayer with me right now, "Father in heaven, I believe that you sent your son, Jesus, to die on the cross for my sins. Forgive me for all of my sins. By faith, I accept his sacrifice for me; I invite him into my heart and surrender my life to him. Thank you for saving me. Amen."

Cynthia Owen and her husband, Joe, are the founders and directors of Christ The Healer Ministries. They have been praying for the sick, teaching people how to receive their healing, and how to walk in their full authority in Christ, since 2001. To contact Cindy, to find more resources in these areas, or to learn about living a new life in Christ, visit the ministry's website at **www.norcalhealing.org**.